Play
Alto Sax
Today!

A Complete
Guide to
the Basics

PLAYBACK+
Speed • Pitch • Balance • Loop

To access audio visit:
www.halleonard.com/mylibrary

Enter Code
3335-5808-7907-6986

ISBN 0-634-02892-8

HAL•LEONARD® CORPORATION
7777 W. BLUEMOUND RD. P.O. BOX 13819 MILWAUKEE, WI 53213

In Australia Contact:
Hal Leonard Australia Pty. Ltd.
4 Lentara Court
Cheltenham, Victoria, 3192 Australia
Email: ausadmin@halleonard.com.au

Visit Hal Leonard Online at
www.halleonard.com

Introduction

Welcome back to *Play Alto Sax Today!*—the series designed to prepare you for any style of saxophone playing, from rock to blues to jazz to classical. The exercises and studies in *Book Two* will help develop your technique, range, and musical abilities. Carefully follow all the suggestions in this book and you'll be well on your way to achieving a professional saxophone sound.

About the Audio

The accompanying audio will make your learning even more enjoyable, as we take you step by step through each lesson and play each song along with a full band. Much as a real lesson, the best way to learn this material is to read and practice a while first on your own, then listen to the track. With *Play Alto Sax Today! Book Two*, you learn at your own pace. If there is ever something that you don't understand the first time through, go back to the audio track and listen again. Every musical track has been given a track number, so if you want to practice a song again, you can find it right away.

Contents

A Quick Review

Posture

Whether sitting on the edge of your chair or standing, you should always keep your:

- Spine straight and tall,
- Shoulders back and relaxed, and
- Feet flat on the floor.

Holding Your Saxophone

- The weight of your instrument should be completely supported by the neck strap. Don't try to hold up the sax with your right thumb. Instead, make sure the neck strap is adjusted so the mouthpiece is exactly at the correct height.

- Keep your fingers arched comfortably, close to the keys. Don't move your hands out of position when using the side keys. Your hands should always be relaxed. Tensing up your hands will limit your dexterity and possibly cause physical damage

Taking Care of Your Instrument

- To remove finger marks from your saxophone, wipe the outside of the instrument with a soft, clean cloth.

- After each practice session, pull the neck swab through the saxophone neck.

- If the neck does not twist easily into the body, clean the tenon with a soft, clean cloth.

- Be careful not to brush the end of the reed against anything because the tip of the reed is very thin and is easily damaged.

- After each practice session, remember to pull the swab through each section of your saxophone. Many experienced saxophone players prefer not to pull a swab through their mouthpieces. A tissue works very well and will not cause abrasions which could adversely effect mouthpiece playing quality.

> ### Warm-ups
>
> Like athletes, musicians need to "warm up" before they perform. A good warm-up will loosen up the muscles of the embouchure and tongue, relax the hands, and focus your mind on playing the instrument. The first three tracks are good warm-up exercises that should be played every day. Before each exercise, take a full and comfortable breath. Work for a smooth, steady tone.

Track 1

Range and Flexibility Builder

Track 2

Technique Trax

Roll the tip of your left thumb up to the octave key. Don't lift it and put it back down. Always remember to keep your thumb on the left thumb key.

Track 3

More Technique Trax

- Be certain that your cheeks don't puff out when you blow.

- For good tone, stretch about half of the red part of your lower lip over your teeth and point your chin downward so it feels long and flat. The reed rests on the outer skin of your lower lip while your upper teeth rest on the top side of the mouthpiece.

- Keep your throat open and your tongue relaxed.

- Blow enough air through your saxophone to produce a full, even tone.

Track 4

Eighth Note March

Eighth Note/Rest

Recall that an eighth note (♪ or ♪) gets ½ of one beat. An equivalent period of silence is represented by an *eighth rest* (𝄾).

Track 5

Minuet

Track 6

Eighth Notes Off the Beat

Eighth Note Scramble

Dancing Melody (New Note: E♭)

El Capitan

Track 7

Track 8

Track 9

Allegro

f

1.

2.

Ready for a quick lesson in music theory? A *scale* is a sequence of notes in ascending or descending order. Like a musical "ladder," each step is the next consecutive note in the key. The scale in the key of G is a specific pattern of **half steps** and **whole steps** (more on this later) between one G and another G an **octave** higher or lower.

The same pattern of half steps and whole steps beginning on a different pitch would produce a different key with a different key signature.

The distance between two pitches is called an *interval*. Starting with "1" on the lower note, count each line and space between the notes. The number of the higher note is the distance of the interval. A whole step or half step is called a **second**, the interval between steps 1 and 3 is called a **third**, and so on. Notice that the interval between scale steps 4 and 6, for example, is also a third.

You already know a sharp raises the pitch of a note. Now you know a sharp raises the pitch of a note by a half-step. Similarly, a flat lowers the pitch of a note one half-step. Two notes that are written differently, but sound the same (and are played with the same fingering) are called enharmonics.

Dark Shadows – E♭/D♯

Notice the D♯ in the second full measure (that is, not counting the partial measure with the pick-up note). It is the same pitch and is played with the same fingering as the E♭ in the fourth measure.

Pick-up note

Notes in Disguise – B♭/A♯

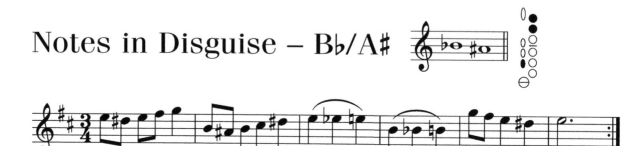

Track 12

Half-Steppin'
(Alternate Fingering: F♯)

Chromatic Scale

At the beginning of this lesson, we saw examples of half steps and whole steps. The smallest distance between two notes is a half-step. A scale made up of consecutive half-steps is called a **chromatic scale**.

Alternate Fingerings

Many notes on the saxophone can be played with more than one fingering. This **alternate fingering** for F♯ should be used whenever it precedes or follows an F♮. Try it both ways and you'll see why using the alternate (or, chromatic) fingering is easier.

Track 13

March Slav

Largo

Largo (lahr' goh) is a tempo indication that means "slow and solemn."

9

Track 14

Egyptian Dance

Look for the enharmonics.

Track 15

Chroma-Zone

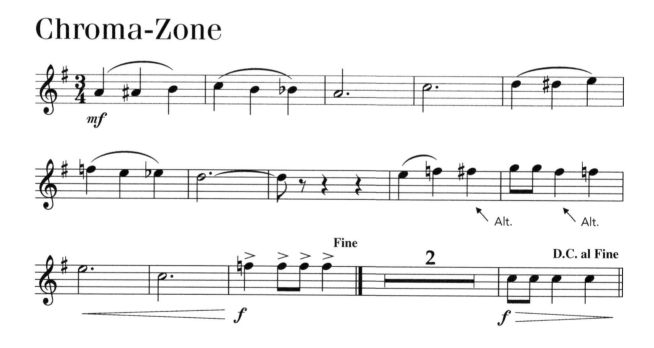

- No two reeds are exactly alike. You may have to try several before you find one that plays well for you.

- Your saliva is alkaline and soon will begin to break down the cellular structure of the reed that enables it to vibrate. Some reeds will last much longer than others.

- A good reed will have a full, rich tone and will play equally well in both the high and low registers.

Track 16

Technique Trax

Track 17

Treading Lightly

Staccato

Staccato (sta kah' to) notes are played lightly and with separation. They are marked with a dot above or below the note. Shorten each note by stopping the air stream.

Track 18

Smooth Move

Tenuto

Tenuto (tih noo' toe) notes are played smoothly and connected, holding each note for its full value until the next is played. They are marked with a straight line above or below the note.

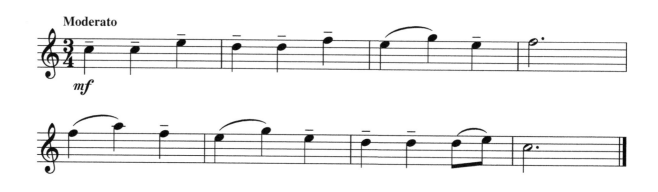

Track 19

Shifting Gears

Track 20

Technique Trax

Track 21

Grandfather's Clock

Track 22

Glow Worm

Allegretto, Ritardando

There are two new terms in this exercise. ***Allegretto*** *(ahl ih gret' toh)* is a tempo indication, usually a little slower than Allegro and with a lighter style. ***Ritardando*** *(rih tar dahn' doh)* means the tempo gradually gets slower. It is usually abbreviated ***rit.*** or ***ritard***.

Paul Lincke

Track 23

Alma Mater (New Note: B)

Always practice long tones on new notes.

Track 24

Loch Lomond

Track 25

Molly Malone

Key Change

The key can change in the middle of a piece. You will usually see a double bar line and a new key signature at the **key change**. You may also see natural signs reminding you to "cancel" previous sharps and flats.

A Cut Above

Alla Breve

Alla Breve (ah' la bra' ve), commonly called **cut time**, has a time signature of ¢ or $\frac{2}{2}$. The top "2" indicates two beats per measure. The bottom "2" means a half note (♩), not a quarter note, gets one beat. Of course, this means a whole note (o) receives two beats and a quarter note (♩) only gets ½ beat.

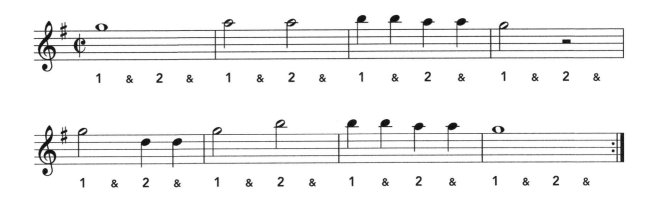

Yankee Doodle

First, play the version in $\frac{2}{4}$. Then repeat the track and play the cut time version. Is there any difference?

The Victors

Notice the 𝅗𝅥. 𝅘𝅥 patterns. In cut time, the dotted half note receives 1½ beats and the quarter note receives ½ beat.

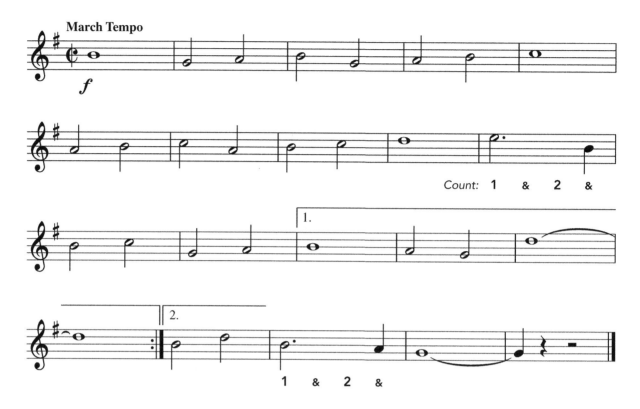

Track 29

A-Roving

Mezzo Piano

We have already seen dynamic markings such as *p*, *mf*, and *f*. **Mezzo piano** (met' zo pee ahn' no), abbreviated *mp*, means moderately soft: a little louder than piano, not as loud as mezzo forte.

Remember to use a full breath support at all dynamic levels.

Track 30

In Sync

Syncopation

Generally, the notes **on** the beat (that's the 1's, 2's, 3's and such) are played a bit stronger or louder than the notes on the **off-beats** (that's the &'s). When an accent or emphasis is given to a note that is not normally on a strong beat, it is called **syncopation**. This sort of "off-beat" feel is common in many popular and classical styles.

Track 31

La Roca

Moderato

Track 32

You're A Grand Old Flag

Rehearsal Numbers

In longer pieces, the publisher sometimes includes *rehearsal numbers* to help the conductor or band leader start and stop the ensemble easily. Sometimes they are letters like A, B, C; sometimes numbers like 1, 2, 3. Frequently, such as here, they are measure numbers.

Crescendo, Decrescendo

A gradual increase in volume is called *crescendo (kreh shen' doh)*. It is usually indicated by *cresc.* or $<$. A corresponding gradual decrease in volume is called *decrescendo (deh kre shen' do)*, abbreviated *decresc.,* or *diminuendo (dih meh nyu ehn' doh)*, abbreviated *dim.* A decrescendo (diminuendo) may be represented by $>$.

George M. Cohan

March Style

Rehearsal number

The Minstrel Boy (New Note: G♯)

This exercise introduces a new key signature: the key of A. Play all F's as F♯, all C's as C♯, and all G's as G♯.

Close Call (New Note: G♯)

Winning Streak

Pay attention to the syncopation. It is similar to what you played earlier, but now the time signature is ¢.

Track 36

Sixteenth Note Fanfare

Sixteenth Notes

A sixteenth note ($\flat$ or $\natural$) has half the value of an eighth note. In $\frac{4}{4}$, $\frac{3}{4}$, or $\frac{2}{4}$ time, four sixteenth notes (♫♫) get one beat.

1 & 2 & 3 e & a 4 &   1 & 2 & 3 e & a 4 &

1 & 2 e & a 3 & 4 &   1 & 2 e & a 3 & 4 &

Track 37

Moving Along

Track 38

Comin' Round The Mountain Variations

Moderato

f

Track 39

Sea Chantey

Observe that an eighth note and two sixteenths are normally written ♪♫. This has the same rhythmic pattern as ♫♪.

Track 40

American Fanfare (New Note: B♭)

Maestoso

Maestoso (mah ee stoh' soh) means "majestic, stately, and dignified."

Track 41

Scale Study

This new key signature indicates the key of F. The first four measures consist of the F scale.

Track 42

Bill Bailey

Moderato

Track 43

Rhythm Etude

Observe that two sixteenth notes followed by an eighth are normally written ♫♪. This has the same rhythmic pattern as ♪♫♫.

Track 44

Celtic Dance

Track 45

The Galway Piper

Track 46

Marching Along

The figures ♪♫♫ and ♪.♫ are equivalent.

S'vivon

Track 47

Moderato

Toreador Song

Track 48

Maestoso

5

13

Lesson 8

Track 49

La Cumparsita

(New Note: E♭/D♯)

The Yellow Rose Of Texas

Track 50

Check the key signature.

Scale Study (New Note: C)

American Patrol

Aria (from Marriage of Figaro)

Track 53

The Stars And Stripes Forever

Track 54

John Philip Sousa

Reproduced by Permission of Boosey & Hawkes Music Publishers Ltd.

Lesson 9

Track 55

Lazy Day

$\frac{6}{8}$ Time

Now you will be introduced to a new time signature: $\frac{6}{8}$. The "6" on top indicates that there are six beats per measure. The "8" on the bottom indicates that the eighth note gets one beat. If the eighth note (♪) gets one beat, then it follows that a dotted quarter note (♩.) receives three beats and a dotted half note (♩.) gets six.

$\frac{6}{8}$ time is usually played with slight emphasis on the 1st and 4th beats of each measure. This divides the measure into two groups of three beats each.

1 2 3 **4** 5 6   **1** 2 3 **4** 5 6   **1** 2 3 **4** 5 6   **1** 2 3 **4** 5 6

Track 56

Row Your Boat

Track 57

Jolly Good Fellow

f — Pick-up on beat 6

28

Track 58

When Johnny Comes Marching Home

In faster music, the primary beats in $\frac{6}{8}$ time (beats 1 and 4) will make the music feel like it's counted in "2," but with a *triple subdivision* of the beat rather than *duple*.

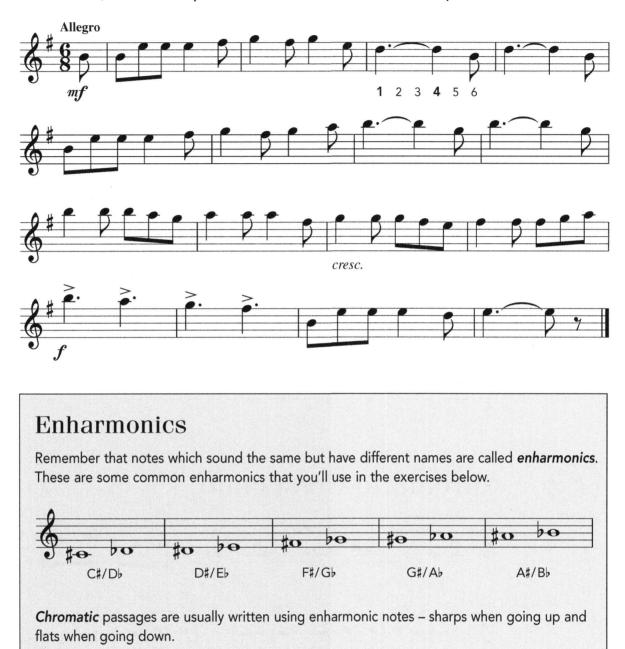

Enharmonics

Remember that notes which sound the same but have different names are called **enharmonics**. These are some common enharmonics that you'll use in the exercises below.

C♯/D♭   D♯/E♭   F♯/G♭   G♯/A♭   A♯/B♭

Chromatic passages are usually written using enharmonic notes – sharps when going up and flats when going down.

Track 59

Chromatic Scale

Practice slowly until you are sure of all the fingerings.

F♯ Alt.

G♭ Alt.

Technique Trax

Track 60

Habañera (from Carmen)

Track 61

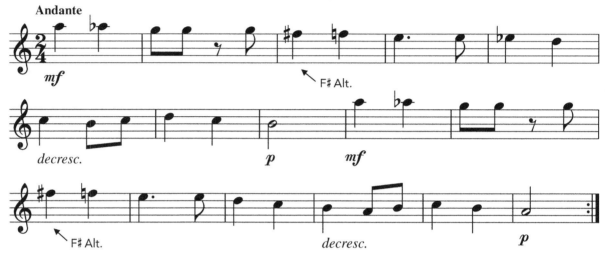

Chromatic Crescendo

Track 62

Staccato Study

Track 63

Track 64

Yankee Doodle Dandy

George M. Cohan

Lesson 10

Track 65

Three To Get Ready

Triplet

A *triplet* is a group of 3 notes played in the time usually occupied by 2. In $\frac{2}{4}$, $\frac{3}{4}$, or $\frac{4}{4}$ time, an eighth note triplet ( ) is spread evenly across one beat.

Track 66

Triplet Study

Theme From Faust

Track 67

Scale Study

New Notes: C#  D

Check Rhythm

Over The River And Through The Woods

On The Move

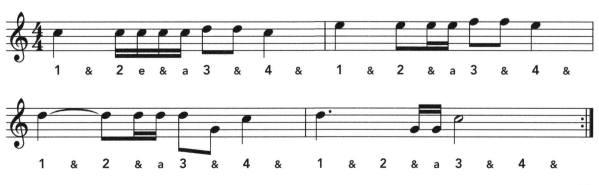

33

Higher Ground

Doodle All Day

Track 72

D.S. March

Track 73

D.S. al Fine

Play until you see **D.S. al Fine**. Then go back to the sign (𝄋) and play until the word **Fine**.
D.S. is the abbreviation for **Dal Segno** (*dahl say' nio*), which is Italian for "from the sign," and
Fine (*fee' nay*) means "the end."

Tarantella

Track 74

Emperor Waltz

Track 75

Andantino

Andantino (ahn dahn tee' noh) is a tempo between Andante and Moderato.

rit.

Unfinished Symphony Theme

Legato

Legato *(leh gah' toh)* means to play in a smooth, graceful manner, almost as if everything was slurred.

Andante

mp legato

Track 77

Greensleeves

Andante

p

mf

rit.

Alto Sax Scales and Arpeggios

Key of C

1.

2.

3.

4.

Alto Sax Scales and Arpeggios

Key of D

1.

2.

3.

4.

Alto Sax Scales and Arpeggios

Key of F

1.

2.

3.

4.

Alto Sax Scales and Arpeggios

Key of A

1.

2.

3.

4.

Fingering Chart for Alto Sax

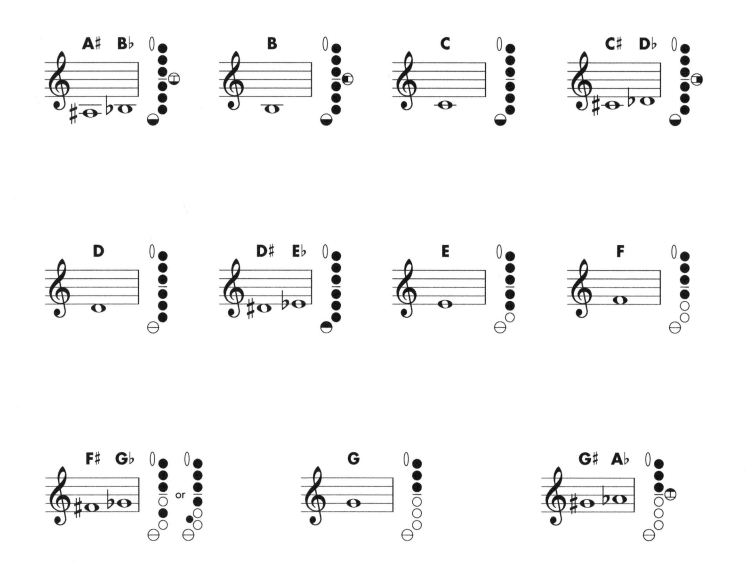

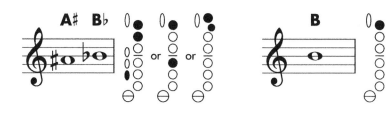

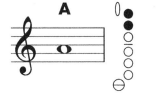

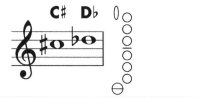

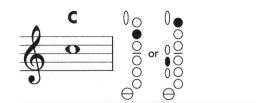

Fingering Chart for Alto Sax

Glossary of Musical Terms

Accent	An Accent mark (>) means you should emphasize the note to which it is attached.
Accidental	Any sharp (♯), flat (♭), or natural (♮) sign that appears in the music but is not in the key signature is called an Accidental.
Alla Breve	Commonly called cut time, has a time signature of ¢ or $\frac{2}{2}$.
Allegretto	A tempo indication usually a little slower than Allegro and with a lighter style.
Allegro	Fast tempo.
Andante	Slower "walking" tempo.
Andantino	A tempo between Andante and Moderato.
Arpeggio	An Arpeggio is a "broken" chord whose notes are played individually.
Bass Clef (𝄢)	(F Clef) indicates the position of note names on a music staff: The fourth line in Bass Clef is F.
Bar Lines	Bar Lines divide the music staff into measures.
Beat	The Beat is the pulse of music, and like a heartbeat it should remain very steady. Counting aloud and foot-tapping help maintain a steady beat.
Breath Mark	The Breath Mark (ʼ) indicates a specific place to inhale. Play the proceeding note for the full length then take a deep, quick breath through your mouth.
Chord	When two or more notes are played together, they form a Chord or harmony.
Chromatic Notes	Chromatic Notes are altered with sharps, flats and natural signs which are not in the key signature.
Chromatic Scale	The smallest distance between two notes is a half-step, and a scale made up of consecutive half-steps is called a Chromatic Scale.
Common Time	Common Time (𝄴) is the same as $\frac{4}{4}$ time signature.
Crescendo	Play gradually louder. (*cresc.*)
D.C. al Fine	D.C. al Fine means to play again from the beginning, stopping at Fine. D.C. is the abbreviation for Da Capo, or "to the beginning," and Fine means "the end."
D.S. al Fine	Play until you see D.S. al Fine. Then go back to the sign (𝄋) and play until the word Fine. D.S. is the abbreviation for Dal Segno, which is Italian for "from the sign," and Fine means "the end."
Decrescendo	Play gradually softer. (*decresc.*)

Diminuendo	Same as decrescendo. (*dim.*)
Dotted Half Note	A note three beats long in duration (♩.). A dot adds half the value of the note.
Dotted Quarter Note	A note one and a half beats long in duration (♩.). A dot adds half the value of the note.
Double Bar (‖)	Indicates the end of a piece of music.
Duet	A composition with two different parts played together.
Dynamics	Dynamics indicate how loud or soft to play a passage of music. Remember to use full breath support to control your tone at all dynamic levels.
Eighth Note	An Eighth Note (♪) receives half the value of a quarter note, that is, half a beat. Two or more eighth notes are usually joined together with a beam, like this: ♫
Eighth Rest	Indicates 1/2 beat of silence. (𝄾)
Embouchure	Your mouth's position on the mouthpiece of the instrument.
Enharmonics	Two notes that are written differently, but sound the same (and played with the same fingering) are called Enharmonics.
Fermata	The Fermata (𝄐) indicates that a note (or rest) is held somewhat longer than normal.
1st & 2nd Endings	The use of 1st and 2nd Endings is a variant on the basic repeat sign. You play through the music to the repeat sign and repeat as always, but the second time through the music, skip the measure or measures under the "first ending" and go directly to the "second ending."
Flat (♭)	Lowers the note a half step and remains in effect for the entire measure.
Forte (𝆑)	Play loudly.
Half Note	A Half Note (♩) receives two beats. It's equal in length to two quarter notes.
Half Rest	The Half Rest (▬) marks two beats of silence.
Harmony	Two or more notes played together. Each combination forms a chord.
Interval	The distance between two pitches is an Interval.
Key Change	When a song changes key you will usually see a double bar line and the new key signature at the key change. You may also see natural signs reminding you to "cancel" previous sharps and flats.
Key Signature	A Key Signature (the group of sharps or flats before the time signature) tells which notes are played as sharps or flats throughout the entire piece.
Largo	Play very slow.

Glossary continued

Ledger Lines	Ledger Lines extend the music staff. Notes on ledger lines can be above or below the staff.
Legato	Legato means to play in a smooth, graceful manner, almost as if everything was slurred.
Mezzo Forte (*mf*)	Play moderately loud.
Mezzo Piano (*mp*)	Play moderately soft.
Moderato	Medium or moderate tempo.
Multiple Measure Rest	The number above the staff tells you how many full measures to rest. Count each measure of rest in sequence. (▬)
Music Staff	The Music Staff has 5 lines and 4 spaces where notes and rests are written.
Natural Sign (♮)	Cancels a flat (♭) or sharp (♯) and remains in effect for the entire measure.
Notes	Notes tell us how high or low to play by their placement on a line or space of the music staff, and how long to play by their shape.
Phrase	A Phrase is a musical "sentence," often 2 or 4 measures long.
Piano (*p*)	Play soft.
Pitch	The highness or lowness of a note which is indicated by the horizontal placement of the note on the music staff.
Pick-Up Notes	One or more notes that come before the first full measure. The beats of Pick-Up Notes are subtracted from the last measure.
Quarter Note	A Quarter Note (♩) receives one beat. There are 4 quarter notes in a $\frac{4}{4}$ measure.
Quarter Rest	The Quarter Rest (𝄽) marks one beat of silence.
Repeat Sign	The Repeat Sign (:‖) means to play once again from the beginning without pause. Repeat the section of music enclosed by the repeat signs (‖: :‖). If 1st and 2nd endings are used, they are played as usual—but go back only to the first repeat sign, not to the beginning.
Rests	Rests tell us to count silent beats.
Rhythm	Rhythm refers to how long, or for how many beats a note lasts.
Ritardando (*rit.*)	Means the tempo gradually gets slower.
Scale	A Scale is a sequence of notes in ascending or descending order. Like a musical "ladder," each step is the next consecutive note in the key signature.
Sharp (♯)	Raises the note a half step and remains in effect for the entire measure.

Sixteenth Note	A sixteenth note (♬ or ♪) has half the value of an eighth note. In $\frac{4}{4}$, $\frac{3}{4}$, or $\frac{2}{4}$ time, four sixteenth notes (♬♬) get one beat.
Slur	A curved line connecting notes of different pitch is called a Slur.
Staccato	Play the notes lightly and with separation.
Tempo	Tempo is the speed of music.
Tempo Markings	Tempo Markings are usually written above the staff, in Italian. (Allegro, Moderato, Andante)
Tenuto	Play the notes smoothly and connected, holding each note for its full value until the next is played.
Tie	A Tie is a curved line connecting two notes of the same pitch. It indicates that instead of playing both notes, you play the first note and hold it for the total time value of both notes.
Time Signature	Indicates how many beats per measure and what kind of note gets one beat.
Treble Clef (𝄞)	(G Clef) indicates the position of note names on a music staff: The second line in Treble Clef is G.
Trio	A Trio is a composition with three parts played together.
Triplet	A triplet is a group of three notes played in the time usually occupied by two. In $\frac{2}{4}$, $\frac{3}{4}$, or $\frac{4}{4}$ time, an eighth note triplet (♫♪) is spread evenly across one beat.
Whole Note	A Whole Note (○) lasts for four full beats (a complete measure in $\frac{4}{4}$ time).
Whole Rest	The Whole Rest (-) indicates a whole measure of silence.